first duet album

for two violins

Compiled, Arranged, and Edited by
HARVEY S. WHISTLER and HERMAN A. HUMMEL

CONTENTS

RUBANK®

HAL•LEONARD®
CORPORATION
7777 W. BLUEMOUND RD. P.O. BOX 13819 MILWAUKEE, WI 53213

First Duet

TOURS

Second Duet

TOURS

Theme and Variation

RIES

Valse Petite

TOURS

Valse Brillante

EICHBERG

Reverie

L. SCHUBERT

Legende

EICHBERG

Sonatine

DANCLA

Valse - Scene

EICHBERG

Duo Caprice

DANCLA

Valse Chromatic

EICHBERG

Duo in G

KALLIWODA

Impromptu

JANSA

Divertimento

PLEYEL

Duo in D

HOFFMANN

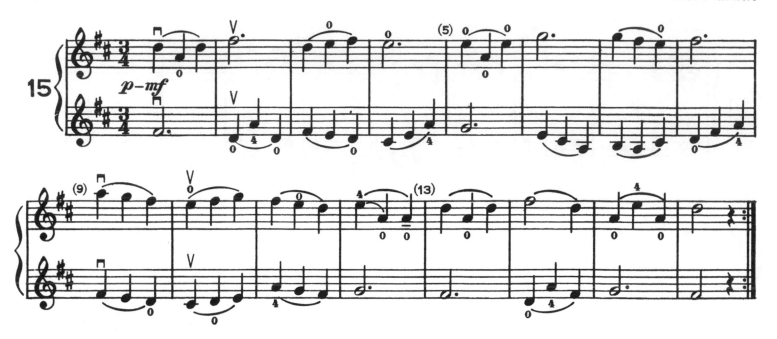

Portrait

GRÜN

★ *Con sordini 1st time*
★ ★ *Senza sordini 2nd time*

★ *Con sordini: With the mutes.*   ★ ★ *Senza sordini: Without the mutes.*

Madrigal

DANCLA

Duo in A

GRÜN

Ballade

GRÜN

Duo de Concert

MAZAS

Duo in F

WOHLFAHRT

Nocturne

MAZAS

Andante Cantabile

PLEYEL

Duo in B♭

VIOTTI

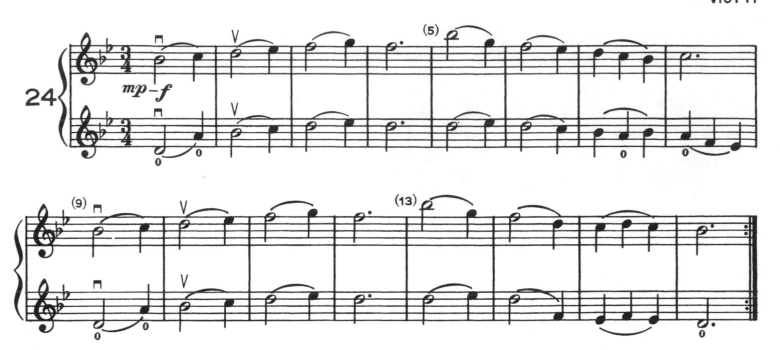

Pizzicato Prelude

DE BERIOT

Romance

MAZAS

Berceuse

PLEYEL

Con sordini 1st time
Senza sordini 2nd time

Scherzo No. 1

WICHTL

Scherzo No. 2

WICHTL

Duettino de Salon

WOHLFAHRT

Valse-Serenade

EICHBERG

Duo Brillante

HOHMANN

Rondo

HOFFMANN

Jubilee

PLEYEL

Canzonetta

EICHBERG

Air Varie

WEISS

Duo Pastorale

MAYSEDER

Duo Majestic

SPOHR

Matineé

EICHBERG

Duo de Ballet

GEBAUER

Allegro Brillante

HENNING

Duo-Finale No. 1

TOURS

Duo-Finale No. 2

TOURS